A
WORKSHOP
ON

The Book of
First Corinthians

Books in the Workshop Series

A Workshop on Self-Giving
by Marilyn Anderes

A Workshop on Bible Marriages
by Diane Brummel Bloem with Robert C. Bloem

A Workshop on the Beatitudes
by Diane Brummel Bloem

A Workshop on The Book of Job
by Diane Brummel Bloem

A Workshop on the Book of Proverbs
by Diane Brummel Bloem

A Workshop on The Sermon on the Mount
by Diane Brummel Bloem

A Workshop on the Book of Colossians
by Margaret and Paul Fromer

A Workshop on the Book of Philippians
by Margaret and Paul Fromer

A Workshop on the Book of Ephesians
by Martha Hook

A Workshop on the Book of John
by Carolyn Nystrom

A Workshop on the Book of Mark
by Carolyn Nystrom

A Workshop on the Book of Romans
by Carolyn Nystrom

A Workshop on the Christian Faith
by Carolyn Nystrom

A Workshop on David and His Psalms
by Carolyn Nystrom

A Workshop on the Book of First Corinthians
by Carolyn Nystrom and Margaret Fromer

A Workshop on the Book of James
by Carolyn Nystrom and Margaret Fromer

A Workshop on Time Management
by Ann Roecker

A Workshop on Worship
by Robert E. Webber

A WORKSHOP ON

The Book of First Corinthians

CAROLYN NYSTROM
MARGARET FROMER

ZondervanPublishingHouse
Grand Rapids, Michigan

A Division of HarperCollins*Publishers*

A WORKSHOP ON THE BOOK OF 1 CORINTHIANS
Copyright © 1985 by The Zondervan Corporation

Previously Published as: People in Turmoil: A Women's Workshop on
1 Corinthians

Requests for information should be addressed to:
Zondervan Publishing House
1415 Lake Drive, S.E.
Grand Rapids, Michigan 49506

Library of Congress Cataloging-in-Publication Data

Nystrom, Carolyn.
    A Workshop on the Book of 1 Corinthians
    Bibliography: p.
    1. Bible. N.T. Corinthians, 1st—Text-books.
I. Fromer, Margaret. II. Title.
BS2675.5.N97   1984   227'.2'0076   84-21013
ISBN 0-310-41891-7

Cover Design by Foster Design Associates

Printed in the United States of America

91 92 93 94 95 / CH / 10 9 8 7 6 5 4 3 2

CONTENTS

THE CHURCH AT CORINTH

James Stalker said, "Paul's letters take the lid off the meeting places of the early Christians and let us look inside." In Paul's letter to the Corinthians, this is perhaps more true than in his other writing. For here we rarely see the lofty theology typical of Paul. Instead we see a shirt-sleeve approach to the nitty-gritty problems of a young church composed of strong-willed people, newly converted from a variety of cultures, and trying, sometimes haltingly, to function as a single body.

Paul first visited Corinth, a buzzing metropolis situated on strategic land and sea routes, in A.D. 50. Midway through his second missionary journey, he had just come from Athens, another Greek city further to the north. There he had discovered a people so fascinated by religion and philosophy that it was no trouble to find an audience in the marketplace. In fact, Athens had been so full of gods that the people had taken steps to be sure no god was inadvertently overlooked:

One altar read *To an unknown god.* Paul used this cultural bridge to preach one of the most concise statements on the nature of God recorded in Scripture. He began, "Now what you worship as unknown, I am going to proclaim to you."

From Athens, Paul continued south, deeper into Greece and eventually came to Corinth. There he met Priscilla and Aquila, fellow tentmakers recently deported from Italy. (Claudius, the emperor, had ordered all Jews out of Rome.) The three tentmakers worked together for a time. Later Silas and Timothy, members of Paul's travel party, came from Macedonia to continue working with him. These five formed a nucleus of Christians ready to evangelize the city of Corinth.

Following his usual plan of action, Paul began at the Jewish synagogue. There he preached that Jesus was the promised Jewish Messiah. When the Jews rejected his message he set up shop in a more fruitful location—next door. The power of his gospel soon became evident. Crispus, the synagogue ruler, and his entire household became converts.

Paul remained at Corinth for at least a year and a half. Many people from all strata of this cosmopolitan city turned to Christ.

In time Paul, accompanied by Priscilla and Aquila, sailed three hundred miles across the Aegean Sea to Ephesus. He stopped briefly there, evidently spotting another fertile field for evangelism, because he left Priscilla and Aquila at Ephesus and promised to return himself. From Ephesus he sailed to Caesarea and probably reported to the mother church in Antioch, thus ending his second missionary journey.

How long he stayed at home, we don't know. The narrative in Acts barely takes a breath before we see Paul setting out once again, this time going almost directly to Ephesus.

In Ephesus, meanwhile, Priscilla and Aquila encountered an educated Jew from Alexandria named Apollos. He preached fervently the beginnings of a Christian message. (He knew about John the Baptist but not about Jesus Christ.) They took him into their home and presented the expanded Christian message to him. Voilà! A new and powerful evangelist. Apollos soon headed across the Aegean to visit the new church at Corinth.

At this point, Paul arrived back in Ephesus to begin a fruitful three-year ministry there. These two cities, Ephesus and Corinth, just a few days' journey across the sea from each other, each enjoyed a lengthy visit from Paul, more time than he spent with any other church.

But all was not well in Corinth. The city was hardly a nurturing environment for the high standards of the Christian faith. In fact, the Corinthians were so immoral that a new phrase, "to Corinthianize," appeared in Greek vocabulary. It came to stand for persons who advocated sexual license. The church, set in this milieu, struggled with many of the issues that face Christians today.

Paul received reports, perhaps from Apollos and definitely from "Chloe's people" (1:11), that the church he had founded some four years earlier was beginning to flounder. Eventually, he received a letter from the church itself, detailing questions about how to settle their spate of problems.

Paul's letter to them, written near the end of his stay at Ephesus, responds to such questions as: How can people who have learned from many strong Christian leaders keep from fighting with each other? How can we balance secular education and spiritual wisdom? Should we pay those who work for the church? What should the church do about members who commit sexual sins? Is our conscience always a safe guide? What should we do about legal disputes between Christians? May a Christian wife leave her non-Christian husband? Should women preach in church? What should we do about competition between Christians with different gifts? Which gifts are most important? Is the Christian life worth the hassle? Is the resurrection of Christ—his physical resurrection—significant to a Christian?

These issues cause as much controversy among Christians now as they did then. And Paul comes to the point of his letter early on: "I appeal to you, brothers, in the name of our Lord Jesus Christ, that all of you agree with one another so that there may be no divisions among you" (1:10). He then proceeds through sixteen chapters to deal with subjects of potential division.

Corinthians is a personal book. It is a practical book. It is also a book of poetic beauty and profound hope. We grew through our study. We trust you will too.

Carolyn and Maggie

I'VE JOINED THE GROUP. NOW WHAT?

You've joined a group of people willing to admit that the Bible is worth studying. Some will admit to far more than that—that the Bible is the Word of God and therefore a standard for day-to-day decisions. Others may say that the Bible is merely a collection of interesting teachings and tales, worthy of time and interest but not much more. You may place yourself at one end of this spectrum or at the other end. Or you may fit somewhere in between. But you have one goal in common with the other people in your group: You believe that the Bible is worth your time, and you hope to enjoy studying it together.

To meet this goal, a few simple guidelines will prevent needless problems.

1. Take a Bible with you. Any modern translation is fine. Suggested versions include: *Revised Standard Version, New American Standard Bible, Today's English Version, New*

International Version, Jerusalem Bible, and *New English Bible.*

A few versions, however, do not work well in group Bible study. For beautiful language, the *King James Version* is unsurpassed. Yours may bear great sentimental value because it belonged to your grandmother. But if you use a *King James Version,* you will spend a great deal of effort translating the Elizabethan English into today's phrasing, perhaps losing valuable meaning in the process.

Paraphrases like the *Living Bible, Phillips,* and *Amplified* are especially helpful in private devotions, but they lack the accuracy of a translation by Bible scholars. Therefore leave these at home on Bible study day.

If you would like to match the phrasing of the questions in this guide, use *The New International Version.* If, however, you fear that any Bible is far too difficult for you to understand, try *Today's English Version.* This easy-to-read translation is certain to change your mind.

2. Arrive at Bible study on time. You'll feel as if you're half a step behind throughout the entire session if you miss the Bible reading and the opening survey questions.

3. Call your host or hostess if you are going to be absent. This saves him or her setting a place for you if refreshments are served. It also frees the group to begin on time without waiting needlessly for you.

4. Volunteer to be a host or hostess. A quick way to feel as if you belong is to have the Bible study group meet at your house.

5. Decide if you are a talker or a listener. This is a discussion Bible study, and for a discussion to work well, all persons should participate more or less equally. If you are a talker, count to ten before answering any question. Try waiting until several other people speak before you give your own point of view.

If you're a listener, remind yourself that just as you benefit from what others say, they profit from your ideas. Besides, your insights will mean more even to you if you put them into words and say them out loud. So take courage and speak.

6. Keep on track. This is a group responsibility. Remember that you are studying the book of 1 Corinthians. Although a sermon, magazine article, or some other book may be related, if brought into the conversation it will automatically take time away from the main object of your study, 1 Corinthians. In the process, the whole group may go off into an interesting but time-consuming tangent, thereby making the leader's job more difficult.

While the Bible is consistent within itself and many excellent topical studies build on its consistency, the purpose of *this* study is to examine thoroughly the book of 1 Corinthians. Therefore cross referencing (comparing sections of 1 Corinthians with other portions of Scripture) will cause the same problems as any other tangent. In addition to confusing people who are unfamiliar with other parts of the Bible, cross referencing may cause you to miss Paul's intent in the passage before you.

You'll find that each paragraph in 1 Corinthians is so laden with facts and ideas that you will be thoroughly challenged to straighten these out without turning to other sections of the Scripture.

Naturally, once you have studied a passage as a group, you may refer back to it. Paul assumed his readers had the earlier passages in mind before they read his next section.

7. Help pace the study. With the questions and your Bible in front of you, you can be aware of whether or not the study is progressing at an adequate pace. Each group member shares the responsibility of seeing that the entire passage is covered and the study brought to a profitable close.

8. Don't criticize another church or religion. You might find that the quiet person across the table attends just that church—and he won't be back to your group.

9. Get to know people in your group. Call each other during the week between meetings. Meet socially, share a car pool when convenient, offer to take in a meal if another group member is ill. You may discover that you have more in common than a willingness to study the Bible. Perhaps you'll add to your list of friends.

10. Invite others to the group. Any Bible study group grows best as it absorbs new people and new ideas. So share your new-found interest with a friend or neighbor.

11. Get ready to lead. It doesn't take a mature Bible student to lead this study. Just asking the questions in this guide should prompt a thorough digging into the passage. Besides, in case you feel a little insecure, you'll find a hefty section of leaders' notes in the back. So once you've attended the group a few times, sign up to lead a discussion. Remember, the leader learns more than anyone else.

ME, A LEADER?

Sure. Many Bible study groups share the responsibility of leading the discussion. Sooner or later your turn will come. Here are a few pointers to quell any rising panic and help you keep the group working together toward its common goals.

1. Prepare well ahead of time. A week or two in advance is not too much. Read the Scripture passage every day for several successive days. Go over the questions, writing out possible answers in your book. Check the Helps for Leaders on pages 99 through 126 for additional ideas, then read the questions again—several times—until the sequence and wording seem natural to you. Don't let yourself be caught during the study with that now-I-wonder-what-comes-next feeling. Take careful note of the major area of application. Try living it for a week. By then you will discover some of the difficulties others in your group will face when they try to do the same. Finally, pray. Ask God to lead you, as you lead the group. Ask Him to make you sensitive to people, to Scripture, and to Himself. Expect to grow. You will.

2. Pace the study. Begin on time. People have come for the purpose of studying the Bible. You don't need to apologize for that. At the appointed hour, simply announce that it is time to begin, open with a prayer, and launch into the study.

Keep an eye on the clock throughout the study. These questions are geared to last for an hour to an hour and fifteen minutes. Don't spend forty-five minutes on the first three questions then have to rush through the rest. On the other hand, if the questions are moving by too quickly, the group is probably not discussing each one thoroughly enough. Slow down. Encourage people to interact with each other's ideas. Be sure they are working through all aspects of the question.

Then end—on time. Many people have other obligations immediately after the study and will appreciate a predictable closing time.

3. Ask; don't tell. This study guide is designed for a discussion moderated by a leader. It is *not* a teacher's guide. When you lead the group, your job is like that of a traffic director. You gauge the flow of discussion, being careful that everyone gets a turn. You decide which topics will be treated in what order. You call a halt now and then to send traffic in a new direction. But you do not mount a soapbox and lecture.

Your job is to help each person in the group discover personally the meaning of the passage and to share that discovery with the others. Naturally, since you have pre- pared the lesson in advance, you will be tempted to tell them all you've learned. Resist this temptation until others have had a chance to discover the same thing. Then, if something is still missing, you may add your own insight to the collection.

4. Avoid tangents. The bane of any discussion group is the oh-so-interesting lure of a tangent. These are always time consuming and rarely as profitable as the planned study. A few red flags will warn you that a tangent is about to arise. They are: "My pastor says . . ."; "I read that . . ."; "The other day Suzie . . ."; "If we look at Ezekiel (or John or Revelation) . . ."

If this occurs, politely listen to the first few sentences. If these confirm your suspicion that a tangent is indeed brewing, thank the person, then firmly but kindly direct attention back into the passage.

A leader does, however, need to be sensitive to pressing needs within a group. On rare occasions the tangent grows out of a need much more important than any preplanned study. In these cases, whisper a quick prayer for guidance, and follow the tangent.

5. Talk about application. Each study in this guide leads to a discussion that applies the point of the passage to real life. If you are short of time or if your group feels hesitant in talking about personal things, you'll entertain the thought of omitting these questions. But if you do, your group will lose the main purpose of the study. If God's Word is a book to live by, a few people in your group ought to be willing to talk about how they are going to live in response to it. Putting those intentions into words will strengthen their ability to live out the teachings. The listeners will be challenged to do the same.

So, always allow adequate time to talk over the application

questions. Be prepared also to share your own experiences as you have tried to live out the passage.

6. Try a prayer 'n' share. Many groups start their session with fifteen minutes of coffee, then hold a short time of sharing personal concerns, needs, and answers to prayer. Afterward, the group members pray briefly for each other, giving thanks and praise, and asking together that God meet the needs expressed. These short, informal sentence prayers are much like casual sharing conversation. The group members simply turn their conversation away from each other and toward God. For many, this brief time of prayer becomes a weekly lifeline.

7. Enjoy leading. It's a big responsibility, but one that is rewarding.

1

WHO IS MY LEADER?

1 Corinthians 1:1–17

"Take me to your leader," says the green-eyed Martian. Enter the myth with him, then put the question in a spiritual context. Where would you take your astral visitor? Would you introduce him to your pastor? A well-known theologian? Or a close friend with whom you confide spiritual secrets?

Who is your spiritual leader? Have you chosen a good one? And are you, by chance, putting too much emphasis on that person's authority?

Read aloud 1 Corinthians 1:1–17.

1. Count the number of times Paul mentions God or the Lord Jesus Christ in these few verses. What impact does this repetition have on you? _____

2. Look again at verses 1–3. How does Paul lay the groundwork for confronting divisions within the Corinthian church? _____

_____

_____

_____

_____

_____

Focus on verses 4–9.

3. a) Who is the active person in these verses?

   b) According to these verses how has God shown His grace to the Corinthians? (Find several ways.) _____

_____

_____

_____

_____

4. Paul says in verse 2 that God has called the Corinthians (and all Christians) to be holy. How might these expressions of God's grace help them do this? _____

_____

_____

_____

_____

5. How do these gifts of God's grace work to tie believers together? _____

_____

_____

_____

6. How might these verses create a desire in you to know and walk with God? _____

_____

_____

_____

Read again verses 10–17.

7. Describe the situation in the Corinthian church that led to Paul's concern. _____

_____

_____

8. What wrong thinking do these divisions reflect? _____

_____

_____

9. What is tempting about following a strong leader? _____

_____

_____

10. Why is it easier to follow an earthly spiritual leader than Christ? _____

_____

_____

Read again verse 17.

11. How can the attraction to a man or his eloquent arguments empty the Cross of its power? _____

_____

_____

_____

12. How might a thorough commitment to Christ as your leader help you form proper relationships with other believers? _____

_____

_____

_____

_____

13. What steps can you take to become a better spiritual leader and a better spiritual follower? _____

_____

_____

_____

_____

2

WHEN IS A WISE PERSON A FOOL?

1 Corinthians 1:18–2:5

Scene: a medieval court.
Character one: a wise king.

He sits on a huge throne overlaid with gold. Peacock-feathered fans, held by slave girls, brush lightly above his head. Another servant stands with a bowl of fruit, waiting his master's desire. The king, hunched in his overgrown chair, mutters words of wisdom that send "oohs" and "ahs" throughout the courtroom, while servants in the doorways rush off to carry out his commands.

Character two: a fool.

The fool, a slave, cavorts nimbly in front of the king, bells tinkling from his pointed cap and shoes. A funny dance step here, a joke there. No one pays him much attention, except the king who occasionally bats an eye.

Everyone present views the king as wise and the fool as—

well, a fool. But God's view of wisdom is different—so different that He might have reversed the characters.

Read aloud 1 Corinthians 1:18–25. Notice the use of the words "foolish," "foolishness," "wise" and "wisdom" in these verses.

1. a) What things are foolish by worldly standards? _____

   _____

   b) What are the characteristics of God's wisdom? _____

   _____

   _____

2. a) How might a person, wise in the world's wisdom, confront sin and human need? _____

   _____

   _____

   _____

   b) How did the Jews expect God to reveal Himself? (Answer from the passage.) _____

   _____

   _____

3. How would the worldly-wise and the Jews be disappointed by a God who died on a cross? _____

   _____

   _____

   _____

   _____

4. Read again Paul's summary statement in verse 25. How does it put the Corinthians' squabbles of verse 12 in perspective? _____

_____

_____

_____

_____

5. When have you experienced God's wisdom to be greater than man's? _____

_____

_____

_____

_____

_____

_____

Read aloud 1:26–31.

6. What things did Paul point to that would help the Corinthians not to overrate earthly wisdom? _____

_____

_____

_____

7. Why did God choose to use people and things outsiders considered weak? _____

_____

_____

_____

8. How does this passage show God's initiative in the spread of the gospel? _____

_____

_____

_____

Read 2:1−5.

9. How did Paul's actions in Corinth set a godly model for the Corinthians? _____

_____

_____

_____

_____

10. Why might it have been harder for the Corinthians to receive Christ if they had been full of earthly wisdom or if Paul had come to them with great eloquence? _____

_____

_____

_____

_____

11. What would a spiritually wise person's attitude be toward himself? _____

_____

God? _____

_____

Christ's death? _____

_____

12. How might Paul's approach to witnessing give you more
freedom to talk about Jesus with others? _____

_____

_____

_____

_____

_____

_____

_____

3

WHAT HAPPENS WHEN GOD GIVES HIMSELF?

1 Corinthians 2:6–3:23

"I follow Paul."
"I follow Apollos."
"I follow Peter."
"I follow Christ."
The Corinthians were entangled in a shouting match: a free-for-all comparable to a small boys' battle of "My daddy is bigger than your daddy."

Paul quells this fracas with an astounding truth: God Almighty has given you Himself. And when God gives Himself, Paul points out, three things happen: 1) He gives each believer the mind of Christ; 2) He plants the Holy Spirit within the local congregation of believers; 3) He gives Christians a relationship of belonging to Him.

And when God has so richly given "all things," a fight over human leaders seems a trifle silly.

Read aloud 1 Corinthians 2:6–16.

1. What are the characteristics of Paul's message of "wisdom"? (Find several in verses 6–10.) _____

    _____

    _____

    _____

    _____

2. What parallels does Paul draw between knowing a person and knowing God? _____

    _____

    _____

    _____

    _____

3. According to these verses, why is the Holy Spirit such a special gift to God's people? _____

    _____

    _____

    _____

4. What hints do you find here that the mind of Christ will sometimes put you out of step with the rest of the world? (Use all of the passage just read.) _____

    _____

    _____

    _____

    _____

5. What positive effects can the mind of Christ have on your day-to-day experience? _____

_____

_____

_____

_____

6. For a moment think of one reason why you value the mind of Christ. Pray a sentence prayer thanking God for this special gift.

Read aloud 3:1–9.

7. Describe the problem that hinders the Corinthians from receiving all the truth Paul could give them. _____

_____

_____

_____

_____

8. How does Paul use the figure of the field in verses 5–9 to show up the superficiality of the Corinthian quarrels? ____

_____

_____

_____

Read aloud verses 10–17.

9. a) Paul now changes his picture of the church from a field to a building. What are the functions of a foundation? _____

_____

_____

b) Review Paul's previous statements about Jesus Christ. (1 Corinthians 1:4–5; 1:21–24; 1:30; 2:16.) According to these verses, why is Christ the essential foundation for the church? _____

_____

_____

_____

_____

10. Paul refers to the local church as "God's temple." What do you see here that shows how important the church is to God? _____

_____

_____

_____

_____

11. If you believe that your local church is as important as Paul says it is, what steps can you take to make it a more habitable place for God's Spirit? _____

_____

_____

_____

_____

Read aloud verses 18–23.

12. According to these verses, how might we deceive ourselves? _____

    _____

    _____

    _____

13. a) What are some of the treasures Paul says you have in Jesus Christ? _____

    _____

    _____

    b) Which of these is most meaningful to you? _____

    _____

    c) Why? _____

    _____

4

WHAT IS A GOOD FATHER?

1 Corinthians 4

If you were writing a job description for the occupation of father, what would you include?

Some of the following actions might head your list: A good father expresses his love for his children; he spends time with them; he provides for their physical and emotional needs; he sets out clear guidelines for behavior; he teaches them moral and spiritual values; he disciplines them wisely and fairly.

Midway through 1 Corinthians 4, Paul describes himself as a father to the Corinthians. He speaks, of course, of a spiritual not a physical family, but it's surprising how similar the father-qualities are. Paul's relationship with the Corinthians provides a measuring stick by which we can check our own spiritual leaders. And if we stand next to that stick ourselves, we might discover how we can better grow under their guidance.

1. In view of the divisions described in 1 Corinthians 1:12, how might the situation at Corinth have become a temptation for Paul? _____

    _____

Read aloud 1 Corinthians 4:1–7.

2. Why does Paul take human judgment, even his own, so casually? (Search all seven verses.) _____

    _____

    _____

    _____

3. What do you learn here about God's judgment? _____

    _____

    _____

    _____

    _____

4. Why might you prefer to be judged by God rather than people? _____

    _____

    _____

    _____

5. How should we regard the gifts of our leaders? _____

    _____

    _____

Read verses 8–13.

6. a) What details did Paul use to caricature the Corinthians (vv. 8–10)? _____

_____

_____

b) How did the Corinthians contrast the apostles to themselves? _____

_____

_____

_____

7. a) Survey Paul's description of himself as an apostle. _____

_____

_____

b) Why would the Corinthians' values make it hard for them to learn from him? _____

_____

_____

8. a) What kind of image would you like your spiritual leaders to present? _____

_____

_____

b) What personal tastes do you have which might get in the way of your hearing spiritual truth? _____

_____

_____

_____

Read aloud verses 14–21.

9. What was Paul doing to fulfill the duties of a loving father? _____

_____

_____

_____

10. What standards do you find in this chapter that would help you evaluate a spiritual leader, one who imitates Paul? (Find at least one from each section: verses 1–7, 8–13, 14–21.) _____

_____

_____

_____

_____

11. a) Make a short list of people whom you consider to be your spiritual leaders. _____

_____

_____

b) Circle one who is particularly important to you.

c) What steps can you take to better benefit from this person's ministry? _____

_____

_____

5

WHO CLEANS HOUSE IN GOD'S CHURCH?

1 Corinthians 5

"Get rid of the old yeast that you may be a new batch without yeast—as you really are."

With these words Paul enters one of the most difficult areas of church government—church discipline. But instead of stony-faced Puritans and witch hunts, Paul paints a picture overshadowed by solemn grief.

Church discipline, no matter how lovingly administered, brings pain—a pain so intense that most churches avoid it entirely. In a perfect church there would be no need for it. But the Corinthian church was not perfect, and neither is ours; so when discipline becomes necessary, Paul commands a stern, "Get rid of the old yeast."

Read aloud 1 Corinthians 5:1–8.

1. Why should the situation at Corinth have caused the church to grieve? _____

_____

_____

_____

2. a) What did the actions of those in the Corinthian church reveal about their attitude toward sin? _____

_____

_____

_____

b) How did their broad-mindedness stand against both community standards and Old Testament teaching? (See Leviticus 20:11.) _____

_____

_____

_____

3. What details of Paul's instructions underscore the solemn nature of the assembly he advises? _____

_____

_____

_____

4. a) How might keeping the incestuous man in the church be a danger both to him and to the church? _____

_____

_____

_____

_____

_____

b) How might excommunication save the man's spirit?

Note: " 'To deliver such a one unto Satan' is an unusual expression. It occurs elsewhere only in 1 Timothy 1:20. It apparently signifies excommunication (see verses 2, 7, 13). The idea underlying this is that outside the church is the sphere of Satan. . . . To be expelled from the Church of Christ is to be delivered over into that region where Satan holds sway." (Leon Morris, *Tyndale New Testament Commentaries,* [Grand Rapids: Eerdmans, 1958], p. 88.)

_____

_____

_____

5. If we took this passage seriously, how might it affect the procedure by which we admit people to church membership? _____

_____

_____

_____

_____

6. What contrasts does Paul draw between the Corinthian attitude toward sin and God's attitude? (See especially verses 6–8.) _____

_____

_____

_____

7. If the whole Christian life is viewed as a festival celebrating deliverance from sin (v. 8), what actions would be appropriate for this kind of celebration? _____

_____

_____

_____

_____

Read aloud verses 9–13.

8. a) How should we treat outsiders differently than we do other Christians? _____

_____

_____

b) Why does Paul make this distinction? (Base your answers on information in the chapter.) _____

_____

_____

9. a) What other sins does Paul say are damaging to the church? _____

_____

_____

b) Why might Paul have included these? _____

_____

_____

10. Quickly review the whole chapter. What responsibilities do believers have for one another? _____

_____

_____

_____

_____

11. How might judging another Christian be an expression of
    love? _____

    _____

    _____

    _____

12. Mention a time when someone's love for you has been
    expressed by challenging your wrong attitudes or ac-
    tions. _____

    _____

    _____

6

TEMPLE ETHICS

1 Corinthians 6

Picture in your mind's eye a temple. Lofty spires, woven tapestries, jeweled artifacts, vaulted open space reaching ever upward. Now imagine that God Himself dwells in this temple of your imagination. What a sacred holy place! How carefully we'd walk through its chambers.

But Paul draws a different picture of God's temple. In 1 Corinthians 3, he speaks of the congregation of believers, the living church, as God's temple. In chapter 6, he becomes even more personal: God's temple is the body of any person who belongs to Him. So we must ask two questions: "Do we deal with other members of our church as though they make up God's temple?" and "Do we treat our own bodies as a temple of the holy God?"

Read aloud 1 Corinthians 5:12–6:8.

1. a) What choices have the Corinthians made about how
to handle disputes among themselves? _____

_____

_____

_____

   b) What actions should they have taken instead? _____

_____

_____

_____

2. What does Paul say here to show that Christians should
judge their own disputes? _____

_____

_____

3. Review 1 Corinthians 1:24b–25, 30; 2:14–16; 3:18–
19a; 5:4–5. How should these previous teachings give
us confidence as we carry out Paul's instructions to
judge our own disputes? _____

_____

_____

_____

_____

4. Why would one Christian going to court against another
Christian indicate "defeat" (v. 7) no matter what the
legal outcome? _____

_____

_____

5. What are some practical steps your church could take to help its people obey this teaching? _____

_____

_____

_____

Read aloud 6:9–11.

6. What experiences had been common in the lives of the people who now belonged to the Corinthian church? ___

_____

_____

_____

7. What contrast do you see between the Corinthians' former position before God and their current one? _____

_____

_____

Read aloud verses 12–20.

8. a) Mention, in order, all the things Paul says in these verses about the body. _____

_____

_____

_____

b) What is their cumulative impact on you? _____

_____

9. What relationship does Paul see between the need for food and the need for sex? _____

_____

_____

_____

_____

10. How does Paul's view of sexual union conflict with contemporary ideas about casual sex? _____

_____

_____

_____

11. Scan verses 11–12. List everything that would help you resist temptation. _____

_____

_____

_____

12. What illustrations does Paul use to emphasize the intimacy of our relationship with Christ? _____

_____

_____

13. How might a growing awareness that your body is the temple of God's Spirit affect your daily activities? _____

_____

_____

_____

14. Paul ends his argument with the command "Therefore honor God with your body." What forms can honoring God with your body take? _____

_____

_____

_____

_____

7

SHOULD I STAY SINGLE? GET MARRIED? STAY MARRIED?

1 Corinthians 7

A husband and wife, each flanked by a lawyer, stand facing each other in court. Both are pale. They try not to catch each other's eye. A few moments later they sign papers and walk away—separately. And divorce statistics climb one more notch.

Does the Christian faith grant immunity from this scenario? No, but it does offer a measure of protection.

But beware. The Christian standards are not popular. In today's era of "me first," people find Paul's steps toward personal stability at cross circuit with their own goals. It seems the Corinthian culture was as hostile to godly values as our own.

Read aloud 1 Corinthians 7.

1. Paul begins this chapter with the words, "Now for the matters you wrote about." What questions do you think

the Corinthians must have asked Paul? _____

_____

_____

_____

_____

Focus on verses 1–9.

2. In what ways do Paul's views of sex and marriage differ from those popular today? _____

_____

_____

_____

_____

_____

3. If from their first acquaintance, a couple accepted the views Paul expresses here, what do you think would be the effects on their marriage? _____

_____

_____

_____

Focus on verses 10–16.

Note on "to the married" (v. 10) and "to the rest" (v. 12): Verses 10–11 refer to marriages where both partners are Christians. Verses 12–14 refer to marriages where one of the partners became a Christian after the marriage.

4. What are Paul's teachings about divorce? _____

_____

_____

_____

_____

Note: When Paul says, "Not I, but the Lord" (v. 10), he refers to the instructions of Jesus regarding divorce. (See Mark 10:5–12 and Matthew 19:6.) In verse 12, Paul says, "I, not the Lord" because Jesus had not given specific teachings on this subject, but Paul inspired by the Holy Spirit (v. 40) does so for the Corinthians.

5. Why might a Christian consider divorcing a non-Christian partner? _____

_____

_____

6. What are the advantages of a Christian staying married to an unbeliever? _____

_____

_____

Focus on verses 17–24.

7. Notice the frequent use of the word "called." What does Paul emphasize by this repetition? _____

_____

_____

_____

8. What does Paul consider to be more important than a believer's circumstances? _____

_____

_____

9. How might a determination to remain where God has
   called you help give more meaning to your present
   situation? (Consider areas such as marriage, job, money,
   social status.) _____

_____

_____

_____

_____

_____

_____

Focus on verses 25–40.

10. According to these verses, what are the values of single
    life? _____

_____

_____

_____

11. a) What influence did "the present crisis" have on Paul's
    advice about marriage? _____

_____

   b) Which of Paul's values of single life remain constant
   even without crisis circumstances? _____

_____

_____

_____

12. If you were deciding whether to marry, what questions would this chapter prompt you to think about? (Try to form one question from each paragraph.) _____

_____

_____

_____

_____

13. a) Think about your own situation, whether married or single. Which teaching of this passage do you need most? _____

_____

   b) How might you begin putting it into action? _____

_____

_____

8

HOW CAN I DEVELOP A HEALTHY CONSCIENCE?

1 Corinthians 8

"You mean you don't have any sense of right and wrong?" A counselor stares at his client with unblinking scrutiny. "No inner nudge that whispers warning or assurance?"

"No, I lost that years ago," his client shrugs carelessly. "I'm liberated."

"But it must be hard for you, with no set ideals, to have to judge each situation on its own merit—isn't it?" the counselor probes. "You have to consider all the possible results of each action every time. Even then you must sometimes wish you'd made a different choice."

His client slumps in silent admission.

The apostle Paul cautions against wounding a weak conscience. It seems he thought that a healthy conscience was worth some cultivation.

Note: "It may seem strange that the Christians in Corinth had trouble seeing that anything to do with idolatry had no place in the life of a Christian. However, the situation was complicated for the new convert by two facts. First, sacrifice was an integral part of social life. Almost any occasion when people came together socially was appropriate for a sacrifice. To stay away from all occasions where there was sacrifice was to be cut off from most social contact. Second, most of the meat sold in the shops had first been offered in sacrifice. Part of the animal was offered on the altar, part went to the priests, and part to the worshippers. The priests customarily sold what they could not use. It would be difficult to know for sure whether the meat you bought had been part of a sacrifice." (Morris, *Tyndale New Testament Commentaries,* pp. 123–124.)

Read aloud 1 Corinthians 8:1–8.

1. What two factions does Paul address in this chapter? Describe each. _____

   _____

   _____

   _____

2. How might verses 1–3 help a person who values knowledge too highly? _____

   _____

   _____

3. What information would help a person decide whether or not to eat meat sacrificed to idols? _____

   _____

   _____

   _____

4. If you had been a pagan worshiping many gods, how would this description of the true God attract you? _____

_____

_____

_____

5. What pitfalls are there in knowing something that others have not yet discovered? _____

_____

_____

_____

6. Paul begins verse 7 with the words, "But not everyone knows this." How might uncertainty about the true nature of idols affect young Christians? (See verse 4 also.)

_____

_____

_____

_____

7. a) What is a conscience supposed to do? _____

_____

_____

_____

b) How might a conscience become defiled if a person acts opposite to what it tells him or her is right? _____

_____

_____

_____

_____

Read aloud verses 9–13.

8. What reasons do these verses give for protecting the conscience of a weak Christian? _____

_____

_____

_____

9. In summary, describe the two kinds of Christians discussed in this chapter. _____

_____

_____

_____

_____

_____

10. In this chapter, what is the relation between knowledge and a mature conscience? _____

_____

_____

11. Paul opens this chapter with the words, "Knowledge puffs up, but love builds up." How can we use both love and knowledge to build up other Christians? _____

_____

_____

_____

_____

12. a) What might *you* do to develop a mature conscience
that helps you feel guilty about the right things? _____

_____

_____

_____

b) How might you help a weaker Christian do the same?

_____

_____

_____

9

RIGHTS AND DISCIPLINE

1 Corinthians 9

"Welcome to the 'me first' generation," announced social commentators as America entered the 1980s. Community colleges sprouted courses in assertiveness training, park districts installed saunas, and the sale of leisure sports equipment soared.

"Take care of yourself; you're the only *me* you have," preached pop psychologists. And marriage after marriage soured as one partner or the other walked away to "find myself."

First Corinthians will not set well with the "me first" generation. In it Paul talks about such unpopular notions as relinquishing personal rights and practicing self-discipline. But Paul is not a reactionary against the easy life. He merely had discovered something more important than "me."

Read aloud 1 Corinthians 9:1–18.

1. a) What are Paul's claims to a respected position among the Corinthians? _____

   _____

   _____

   b) What is the force of each? _____

   _____

   _____

   _____

2. What are the rights Paul could claim as an apostle? _____

   _____

   _____

   _____

   _____

3. How might making use of these rights help further Paul's itinerant ministry? _____

   _____

   _____

4. What illustrations from social custom and from Scripture does Paul use to establish his right to financial support? __

   _____

   _____

5. How does Paul's discussion here about the rights of an apostle relate to the problems of chapter 8? _____

   _____

   _____

6. Why did Paul voluntarily relinquish some of these rights during his stay at Corinth? _____

_____

_____

_____

7. a) Paul outlines the rights that accompanied his work as apostle. As you consider your major occupation, what rights do you think ought to accompany this position? (Sometimes a sense of irritation is a clue that we feel our rights have been overlooked.) _____

_____

_____

_____

b) Which of these rights ought you to consider relinquishing because of someone else's need? Why? _____

_____

_____

_____

Read aloud verses 19–23.

8. a) How is Paul's overriding desire emphasized in these verses? (Look for repetitions.) _____

_____

_____

_____

_____

b) What effect did this goal have on Paul's relations to other people? _____

_____

_____

9. a) What is unappealing about the job of taking on so many different roles? _____

_____

_____

b) What would make it worthwhile? _____

_____

_____

Read aloud verses 24–27.

10. a) What do you learn about personal discipline from this paragraph?

_____

_____

Note: "Paul fears that *after preaching to others,* like the herald at the games proclaiming the rules of the contest and calling the competitors together, he himself should be *disqualified.* . . . His own salvation is not in question, but his reward for acceptable service. Compare with 1 Corinthians 3:15." (Norman Hillyer, "1 Corinthians," *New Bible Commentary,* [Downers Grove: InterVarsity Press, 1970], p.1063.)

b) What does a person in physical training demand of him or herself? _____

_____

_____

11. How does self-discipline help a Christian avoid being the stumbling block described in chapter 8? _____

_____

_____

_____

12. If you share Paul's goals to help weak Christians and bring others to Christ, what forms of discipline should you institute in your life? _____

_____

_____

_____

_____

10

DO *ALL* TO THE GLORY OF GOD?

1 Corinthians 10

"That dessert looks so tempting," a guest compliments her hostess.

"Temptation? I love it," laughs an office worker. "That's where all the action is."

The Devil Made Me Do It brags a small boy's T-shirt.

Is temptation the harmless fun these comments imply? Or is there a treacherous sucking quality to temptation, like quicksand covered by bright green turf?

In 1 Corinthians 10, Paul speaks of temptation, then goes on to wrap up this three-chapter section on the relationship between personal freedom and Christian responsibility. Then he ends with a challenging goal for all of a believer's actions: the glory of God.

Note: In this passage the New Testament makes one of the clearest statements about the preexistence of Christ: "The rock was Christ" (verse 3). "Rock" is the title commonly given to God in the Old Testament. Used here it is a statement of Christ as the source of all of the people's blessing.

Read aloud 1 Corinthians 10:1–10.

As you read, notice the references to "all," "most," and "some" of the people.

1. a) What happened to each of these groups? _____

_____

_____

_____

   b) How would you expect people who had experienced God so directly to act? _____

_____

_____

2. Why does Paul think it important for the Corinthians not to be ignorant of this ancient history? _____

_____

_____

3. a) According to Paul's brief summary of Hebrew history, what are some of the signs that they were not wholeheartedly set on God? _____

_____

_____

_____

   b) How does each of these acts reveal resistance to God?

_____

_____

_____

4. a) Why might these people have begun to take God for granted? (Look back at the first five verses.) _____

_____

_____

_____

b) What circumstances in your life might cause you to take God for granted? _____

_____

_____

_____

Read aloud verses 11–13.

5. What warnings and comfort do you find mixed in Paul's statements about temptation? _____

_____

_____

_____

6. In your reading so far, what are the indications that temptation cannot be viewed complacently? (Include verse 13.)

_____

_____

_____

7. a) When you are tempted, how might the truths of verse 13 encourage you? _____

_____

_____

b) How might you misuse them? _____

_____

_____

_____

Read aloud verses 14–22.

8. How is the ceremony of Communion a larger act than simply eating and drinking? _____

_____

_____

_____

9. What parallels does Paul draw between the ceremony of Communion and eating food offered to idols? _____

_____

_____

Read aloud 10:23–11:1.

10. Notice that this section is a wrap-up of all Paul has said in chapters 8–10. How does this final section limit the personal freedom described by the repeated words, "Everything is permissible"? _____

_____

_____

_____

_____

11. Why is behavior in an unbeliever's house a question both of good manners and good conscience? _____

    _____

    _____

    _____

    _____

12. a) What does Paul suggest as valid goals for our behavior? (See verses 24, 26, 31, and 33 particularly.) _____

    _____

    _____

    _____

    _____

    b) What do these goals imply about the priorities God wants His people to live by? _____

    _____

    _____

    _____

    _____

13. a) Jot a quick list of all that you have to do yet today. (Tomorrow if you are meeting late in the day.) _____

    _____

    _____

    _____

    _____

Now silently read your list, keeping in mind Paul's words, "So whether you eat or drink or whatever you do, do it all for the glory of God."

    b) What changes in your attitudes or actions would help you perform each of these activities for God's glory? ___

_____

_____

_____

_____

_____

_____

    c) If you could perform each of these jobs with the glory of God as your primary goal, what benefits do you think would result? _____

_____

_____

_____

11

PRIVATE BATTLES WITH PUBLIC WORSHIP

1 Corinthians 11

Why do you go to church? And what do you think about once you are there? Disciplining oneself to worship can be a struggle. But merely getting to church is only half of that battle.

The Corinthians met regularly for public worship, yet their manner of worship was not pleasing to God. As a dutiful spiritual father, Paul took them to task. At the same time, he provided us the opportunity to evaluate our own patterns of public worship.

Read aloud 1 Corinthians 11:1–16.

1. a) What privileges of public worship did Paul assume that men and women share? _____

_____

_____

b) How did Paul say Corinthian men and women ought to worship differently from each other? _____

_____

_____

Note: Corinth was a Greek city, yet it incorporated people of many nationalities. Naturally their customs mingled and sometimes clashed. In worship, for example, Romans and Jews (both men and women according to some scholars) prayed with their heads covered. But Greeks sacrificed to their idols bareheaded.

Socially, women who appeared in public without a veil were viewed as prostitutes (and frequently were). And a woman convicted of sexual immorality would have her head shaved as a punishment.

In a city with such divergent customs, the new Christian church needed guidelines on how to dress for public worship. Beyond that, they needed to form underlying principles to govern future decisions.

2. How might ignoring Paul's instructions hinder the Corinthian church's witness in its community? (How might it reflect on the woman's honor? On her husband's honor? How might it bring dishonor to God?) _____

_____

_____

_____

3. What areas of authority did Paul appeal to in making the point that women in this church should cover their heads? _____

_____

_____

_____

_____

4. What is a wholesome relation between men and women based on the teachings of verses 3, 8–9, and 11? _____

_____

_____

_____

_____

5. With this passage in mind, what underlying principles ought we to consider in our own worship practices? _____

_____

_____

_____

_____

6. What effect do you think this passage should have on a Christian's participation in the current women's movement? _____

_____

_____

_____

_____

Read aloud verses 17–34.

7. If you had attended a typical Communion service at the Corinthian church, what would you have seen and heard? _____

_____

_____

_____

8. What words would you use to describe their attitude? __

_____

_____

9. What indications in verses 23–26 show that Christ's death was more than a martyr's death? _____

_____

_____

_____

_____

10. How would you be affected if you "heard" Jesus say to you directly and personally, "My death is for you"? _____

_____

_____

_____

11. What would be involved in participating in the Lord's Supper in a worthy manner? _____

_____

_____

_____

_____

_____

_____

12. What might be the results of taking Communion unworthily (as the Corinthians did)? _____

    _____

    _____

13. a) In this chapter Paul called the Corinthians to task for the way they worshiped as a group. Review briefly your own thoughts and actions during the last worship service that you attended. _____

    _____

    _____

    b) What does this reveal about the value you place on your own worship of God during a public service? ____

    _____

    _____

    c) What could you do to make your worship in church more acceptable to God? _____

    _____

    _____

    _____

    _____

12

BODY LANGUAGE

1 Corinthians 12

Setting: a church business meeting.

An intense man argues that, for the sake of our older people, we must make better lights in the parking lot a top priority. When his motion is tabled and sent to committee, he walks out of church—and never returns.

A woman, startled by a proposal to "sell those back four lots to raise money for a Christian education wing," shouts, "No one in his right mind is selling land in today's market." Weeks later, we notice she has not reappeared in worship services.

A man dedicated to solving the problem of books "lost" from the church library, makes a plea for a more stern loan policy. When others disagree, saying that the books ought to be available to anyone for any period of time, he changes the lock on the library door, pockets the key, and leaves—for good.

Large issues and small ones (often small issues fronted for hidden larger issues). But sometime during the airing of those differences a tragic event occurred in the life of the church. A single person said inside, "I don't need you; I don't belong." And separation took place.

It's a decision not to take lightly. Paul says, a living body might just as easily lose a hand, or a leg, or an eye.

Read aloud 1 Corinthians 12:1–11.

1. a) What did Paul want the Corinthians, who had just moved out of paganism, to know about the Spirit of God? _____

   _____

   _____

   _____

   b) Why might each of these facts about the Holy Spirit be important? _____

   _____

   _____

   _____

2. If you are a Christian, what must necessarily be true of you according to these verses? _____

   _____

   _____

   _____

3. According to the passage, how might you be different from other Christians? _____

   _____

_____

_____

_____

4. a) List all the gifts mentioned in verses 7–11 and 27–30.

   _____

   _____

   _____

   b) How might you go about discovering your gift? _____

   _____

   _____

   _____

Note: This is a representative, not a comprehensive, list of spiritual gifts. Other lists appear elsewhere in Scripture. Even if all were combined, it would probably not be a complete expression of God's gifts to His people.

5. If all Christians have gifts from the Holy Spirit, one of the gifts listed here might be yours. What might make it hard for you to acknowledge that you have a gift from God? __

   _____

   _____

   _____

6. Why is there no place for pride or jealousy in the church? _____

   _____

   _____

Read aloud verses 12–31.

7. Why does Paul introduce this picture of the human body? _____

_____

_____

8. Compare verse 15 with verse 21. Describe the problems Paul anticipates arising in a fellowship. _____

_____

_____

_____

_____

9. a) Mention a specific job you could not have done today if your foot had refused to function because it was not a hand. _____

_____

   b) Which jobs serve as the hands and feet within your church? _____

_____

_____

   c) What problems might arise if the people performing these jobs behaved as the foot did in verses 14–20? __

_____

_____

_____

_____

10. How, according to verses 21–26, ought the church to regard the less showy gifts? _____

_____

_____

11. a) According to these verses (12–26), what is the basic reason that we fail to suffer with those who suffer and rejoice with those who receive honor? _____

_____

_____

_____

b) What does this chapter say to the person who thinks, "I don't need a church"? _____

_____

_____

_____

12. Look at verses 3 and 27. How is the confession "Jesus is Lord" fundamental to an understanding of diverse spiritual gifts? _____

_____

_____

_____

_____

13

IS MY LOVE GOD'S LOVE?

1 Corinthians 13

Tucked unobtrusively near the end of this practical book about the inner workings of the church lies one of the most beautiful poems in all of Scripture. No introduction is adequate for this chapter, it speaks eloquently for itself.

Read aloud 1 Corinthians 13.

1. What words would you use to describe the emotional impact this passage has on you? _____

_____

2. a) In verses 1–3, what spiritual gifts does Paul use as examples? _____

_____

_____

b) What acclaim might come to a person using these gifts? _____

_____

_____

_____

3. a) How does God rate these gifts? _____

_____

b) How can you reconcile this with Paul's emphasis on gifts in chapter 12? _____

_____

_____

_____

4. What does a person with each of these gifts lose if he or she does not exercise them with love? (Answer for each set of gifts Paul mentioned.) _____

_____

_____

_____

5. a) Take a quick mental survey of your skills and gifts. Which one of these are you likely to offer to God? ____

_____

b) Imagine a situation where you were exercising this gift without love. What would be the results? _____

_____

_____

_____

Read aloud verses 4–7.

Note the descriptions of what love is and what it is not. How are these descriptions grouped? _____

_____

6. a) How are patience and kindness alike? _____

_____

_____

b) How are they different? _____

_____

_____

c) In what circumstances with other Christians might you need one or the other? _____

_____

_____

_____

7. Review each phrase that describes what love is not. How is each of these the opposite of love? _____

_____

_____

_____

_____

_____

_____

8. Look again at verses 6–7. How could you obey these verses and yet not be blind to reality? _____

_____

_____

_____

_____

9. a) Think of a fellow Christian to whom God wants you to be more loving. With this person in mind, read verses 4–7 silently and prayerfully using your own name in place of the word "love."

   b) Now spend a few moments in silent prayer confessing to God specific ways in which you fall short of His definition of love. Ask His forgiveness.

Read aloud verses 8–13.

10. What contrasts do you find in these verses between our present situation and the time to come? _____

_____

_____

_____

_____

_____

11. a) Why will the gifts mentioned in verse 8 not be needed when we see Jesus face to face? _____

_____

_____

_____

   b) Why is love more enduring? _____

_____

_____

12. What comfort is it to know that you'll see Jesus face to
    face and know and be fully known? _____

    _____

    _____

    _____

14

AM I GOD'S GIFT TO MY CHURCH?

1 Corinthians 14

"Do you mean to tell me that not one pair of shoes in this house fits you?" I stared incredulously at my obviously growing nine-year-old son who stood tall in his only surviving pair of raggy sneakers.

"Yip."

My smaller son, Craig, sat, slightly disgruntled and surrounded by several pairs of mostly worn-out shoes, his inheritance in our periodic game of Shift Your Shoes. He could already see the next scene in his mind.

Sure enough, a day later, in marched older brother with a brand new pair of K-Mart hiking boots. "Hey, see my new shoes mom just bought?" (Both boys had been ogling hiking boots for months.) "See all that tire tread on the bottom?"

All evening those spanking new brown boots with red ties flashed around the living room along with equally obvious comments. "Too bad all those old shoes fit you." And "Don't you wish you had new hiking boots?"

That gift of new shoes didn't do much for our family harmony. I was soon tempted to get rid of a certain pair of hiking boots.

Paul noted a similar problem in the highly gifted Corinthian church. But he didn't tell them to stifle their gifts. Instead he leads off chapter 14 by saying they should "eagerly desire spiritual gifts." But he cautions, "Follow the way of love."

Read aloud 1 Corinthians 14:1–12.

1. How would you describe Paul's attitude toward the gift of prophecy? (Answer from verses 1–5.) _____

_____

_____

2. a) What illustrations does Paul use to emphasize his teaching about gifts? (See verses 6–12.) _____

_____

_____

b) What is the main purpose of each illustration? _____

_____

_____

_____

_____

3. What values does Paul want the Corinthians to develop?

_____

_____

_____

4. If one of your primary goals were to build up the church, what effect might this have on the way you now use your gifts? _____

_____

_____

Read aloud verses 13–19.

5. How would you describe Paul's attitude toward the gift of tongues? _____

_____

_____

6. What part does Paul say both mind and spirit play in worshiping God? _____

_____

_____

7. What would be missing if you worshiped with your spirit alone? _____

_____

_____

With your mind alone? _____

_____

_____

Read aloud verses 20–25.

8. a) With what you know of the Corinthians' use of spiritual gifts, how is their thinking like children? _____

_____

_____

_____

b) What guidelines does Paul give here for thinking in a
more mature manner? _____

_____

_____

_____

_____

9. a) If an unbeliever visited your church service, what
would he or she likely think and feel? _____

_____

_____

_____

b) Read again verses 24 and 25. What changes would
have to occur in your church for an unbeliever to be
affected in this way? _____

_____

_____

_____

_____

Read verses 26–40.

10. If you were to have visited a Corinthian worship service
that functioned the way Paul prescribes, what would you
have seen and heard? _____

_____

_____

11. a) How do you think you'd feel as you participated? _____

_____

_____

b) How would it aid you to worship with your mind and spirit? _____

_____

_____

_____

12. What does Paul teach about the purposes of a worship service? (Review the whole chapter.) _____

_____

_____

_____

_____

13. a) Which of these purposes of the worship service are weak in your own church? _____

_____

b) What suggestions might you make to help your church better fulfill this function of worship? _____

_____

_____

_____

_____

_____

15

HOW WILL IT END?

1 Corinthians 15

But what difference will it make if I'm a Christian or if I'm not a Christian? Even if I live until I'm ninety, so what? A hundred years later no one will ever know I existed, let alone whether I belonged to Jesus Christ. Or will they?

The Bible says that God has a special future for His people. It has something to do with Jesus Christ, raised from the dead, being the "firstfruits." In God's Book, the end is merely the beginning.

Read aloud 1 Corinthians 15:1–11.

1. a) When Paul reminded the Corinthians of the gospel to which they had committed themselves, what words stand out as basic beliefs? (See especially verses 3–5.)

_____

_____

b) Why are each of these words important to the Christian creed? _____

_____

_____

_____

2. What evidence did Paul offer first-century Christians who might have begun to doubt Christ's resurrection? ___

_____

_____

_____

Read aloud verses 12–19. *(Circle the word "if" each time Paul uses it to question whether the dead are raised.)*

3. If people who are dead do not live again, what would be the results? Find all that you can from these verses. _____

_____

_____

_____

_____

_____

4. If it were true that there is no life after death, why would a Christian deserve pity? _____

_____

_____

_____

Read aloud verses 20–34.

  5. In what sense is Christ the "firstfruits"? _____

_____

_____

_____

  6. What future events does this passage detail? _____

_____

_____

_____

_____

  7. How might this revelation of the future help you to worship God? _____

_____

_____

_____

  8. Paul says in verses 33–34, "Do not be misled. . . . Come back to your senses." This is a plea for the Corinthians to return to their former faith in the Resurrection. (See verses 11–12.) What effect would belief or lack of belief in the Resurrection have on behavior? _____

_____

_____

_____

_____

_____

Note on "baptized for the dead" (verse 29): The Greek text may also be translated, "baptized because of the dead." *The dead* may refer to Jesus Christ, or it might refer to Christian friends who had died but had influenced others to follow them in faith and baptism.

9. When you visualize a resurrection from the dead, what problems come to your mind? _____

_____

_____

_____

Read aloud verses 35–58.

10. What does the example of a seed contribute to your understanding of life after death? _____

_____

_____

_____

_____

11. a) What two sources of life does Paul point out? (See verses 44–49.) _____

_____

b) What do we inherit from each? _____

_____

_____

_____

Note: "Last Adam" (v. 45) is Jesus Christ.

12. According to Paul, how will life as we know it end? _____

_____

_____

_____

_____

_____

13. Look again at verses 55–58. What does Paul suggest are natural outgrowths of the Christian view of resurrection?

_____

_____

14. If you were to encounter a period of wavering faith, how might this chapter help you stand firm? _____

_____

_____

_____

_____

15. If this belief in the Resurrection motivated you to "give yourself fully to the work of the Lord" (v. 58), what specific influences would you see on your own work and service? _____

_____

_____

16

UNTIL I COME . . .

1 Corinthians 16

Paul finishes his letter to the church at Corinth with a few personal notes. At first glance they seem fragmented, sort of like a series of postscripts. But on closer inspection we see that Paul allowed us an intimate glimpse of himself, the people who work with him, his plans for the future—as well as his parting concerns for the church he had planted at Corinth.

And even though he has written a letter of instruction sixteen chapters long, Paul isn't finished yet with the Corinthians. His final notes include words bound to spur a reluctant church into action: "I hope to spend some time with you." Reason enough for a wayward church to take seriously the letter's content.

Read aloud 1 Corinthians 16:1–12.

1. a) What are Paul's plans for himself? _____

    _____

    _____

   b) What are his expectations for the Corinthians until he sees them again? _____

    _____

    _____

2. a) In what variety of ways does Paul show his concern for the church at Jerusalem? _____

    _____

    _____

   b) What are the advantages to the Corinthians in collecting money the way Paul suggested? _____

    _____

    _____

    _____

    _____

3. As you consider your own giving, how might you benefit from these principles? _____

    _____

    _____

    _____

4. In verses 8–9, Paul indicates that there is a lot going on in his ministry in Ephesus. Read Acts 19:8–20 for a sample of his work there.

a) What do you think were the positive effects of the opposition on his work? _____

_____

_____

_____

b) How might knowing this encourage you to take risks in serving God? _____

_____

_____

_____

5. Considering what you know of the Corinthians, why might Paul have been concerned about young Timothy's stay in Corinth? _____

_____

_____

_____

_____

Read verses 13–24.

6. a) What final commands did Paul leave with the Corinthians? _____

_____

_____

b) How might obeying these commands have helped to solve the Corinthian problems that have become apparent throughout this letter? _____

_____

_____

_____

_____

7. a) How is Stephanas an illustration of Paul's command to do everything in love? _____

_____

_____

_____

b) In what other ways does Paul encourage love in these verses? _____

_____

_____

_____

8. a) Examine your own relations with other Christians. How do they know that you care about them? _____

_____

_____

_____

b) How can you use the examples in these verses to better express your love? _____

_____

_____

_____

9. As you look back over Paul's letter to the Corinthians, what good qualities do you find in this church? _____

_____

_____

_____

_____

10. What weaknesses would you like your church to avoid?

_____

_____

_____

11. How can Paul's instructions to the Corinthians make your church more pleasing to God? _____

_____

_____

_____

_____

_____

HELPS FOR LEADERS

1 / WHO IS MY LEADER?

1 Corinthians 1:1–17

Q2. Involve as many group members as possible. If your group is accustomed to single-answer study questions, use this question to help them adjust to multiple answers. Keep asking for more until they have picked out most of the following answers:

— Paul says he is an *apostle* (v. 1).
— He claims apostleship *by the will of God* (v. 1).
— He points out that the Corinthian church is *God's church* (v. 2).
— He says they *all* have God's call to be holy *together* (v. 2).
— Holiness is not unique to them; it is to *all everywhere* who call on Jesus (v. 2).
— Jesus is their Lord and *ours* (v. 2).

— God is *our* Father (v. 3)

In summary, Paul points out that they are all (including himself) in the same family, under the same authority, within the same church, and subject to the same call.

Q3. Encourage participants to find as many answers as possible since succeeding questions depend on a thorough answer here. Someone may notice that verse 9 assumes that the graces from God all form evidence that God is faithful.

Q5. Use the answers from the previous two questions to draw conclusions here. Group members should notice that we have a future together (v. 8), we have a fellowship together (v. 9), our gifts and goals are the same (holiness, fellowship, waiting), we need to depend on each other and on God for knowledge and speaking gifts (v. 5). In addition, the fact that our focus is on Jesus Christ ties us together—our enthusiasm is for the same person.

Q6. Wait long enough for most of the group members to respond to this question.

Q8. The crux of this wrong thinking rests on an overemphasis of human spiritual leaders. Paul tackles this head on in verses 13 and 14.

Additional discussion might reveal that some Corinthians must have thought Christ no more than equal with "other great men." They emphasized too much the power and attraction of human leaders rather than Christ and the cross of Christ. Even Paul's being sent to *preach,* not to baptize (and his humorous forgetfulness about whom he did and did not baptize) puts a more correct emphasis on the message rather than the preacher.

Q11. This question calls for interpretation of Paul's final phrase in today's passage. Encourage group members to discuss possible meanings.

They will likely discover that an overemphasis on human leaders causes people to follow each other—not Jesus Christ.

This may result in false conversions with a change in lifestyle, but no heart commitment to Jesus Christ as Savior from sin and Lord of life. Once the human leader leaves (or reveals his own human weaknesses), the "convert" returns to his former ways. Furthermore, he may be immune to any further message of the gospel. For him, the cross of Christ has been emptied of its power. He's tried it already.

Don't skimp on understanding the concept behind this question since next week's study builds on this basis.

Q12, Q13. Encourage most group members to participate in these final questions of application.

2 / WHEN IS A WISE PERSON A FOOL?

1 Corinthians 1:18—2:5

Q1. a) Have the group members scan the passage again, picking out the words and phrases that answer this question in order of their occurrence. Answers should come from as many people as possible, so that all begin to be involved in the discussion.

b) Find as many answers as possible from the passage. Some characteristics of God's wisdom are 1) in its difference from what people commonly believe to be wise, 2) in its spread by preaching, and 3) in its content and results: the Cross, a crucified Savior, and rescue for those "foolish" enough to believe. Those who believe God's wisdom is foolish will perish.

Q2. a) This question is one that calls on the imagination of group members. Some answers might fall in the areas of power, wealth, education, or good government.

b) The Jews demanded signs of power and a Messiah who would live to rule, not die ignominiously on a cross.

Q3. First, it isn't even sensible to think that a *dead* god can be effective. Second, a corpse has no power to make wrongs right. God's answer seems neither wise nor powerful as we think of wisdom and power.

Q4. The Corinthians' argument makes Christ just another man like Paul or Apollos or Cephas. But in fact, He is uniquely God's man. God's answer is found in Him alone and in no other. Others are merely messengers regardless of their wisdom, attractiveness, or holiness.

Q5. Some of the members of your group have undoubtedly had experiences that would be appropriate to share now. Watch the amount of time given to this so that you have time to finish the study without rushing.

Q6. Paul primarily points to the Corinthians' own experience. There aren't very many of them who have been considered wise, influential, or noble. Yet they are the very ones who have been given the privilege of understanding God's wisdom. God's wisdom has to do with righteousness, holiness, and redemption.

Q7. All the credit is to belong to God; not to the eloquence of a John Wesley or the wisdom of a Paul or the attractiveness of a pastor or to our own intelligence in figuring things out. It is to be God's alone.

Q8. The passage emphasizes God's choice and calling and contrasts this to the weakness and inability of those who were chosen and called.

Q9. Paul did not use showmanship or convincing logic to win the Corinthians, but allowed the Spirit of God to be on display, so that they could begin to learn to trust God's power and wisdom and not their own.

Q10, Q11. These two questions, though they encourage the group to be imaginative, are based on the passage. Each person responding should be able to indicate what information in the passage gave rise to his or her response.

Q12. Encourage personal response in this application question.

3 / WHAT HAPPENS WHEN GOD GIVES HIMSELF

1 Corinthians 2:6–3:23

Q2. Using verses 10–16, think first about how people know each other. (What can they know and not know?) Then discuss the way they can know God. (Who knows God? Who cannot know God? What makes the difference?) Finally, compare and contrast knowing each other with knowing God.

Q3. See particularly verse 12.

Q4. Participants should find several answers in these verses. Be sure someone points out that when we receive the Spirit of God (v. 12), we also receive the mind of Christ (v. 16). Since Christ was out of step with this world (enough to be crucified), we may find ways we are different from the world. But what better way to know a person than to have *his mind* in us?

Q5. Aim for each person to respond in some way. Areas you might consider include your relationship with family members, your plans for the future, the way you behave in a stressful situation, the use you make of your intelligence and skills, the way you view material things, your practice of worship.

Q6. If your group has discussed question 5 thoroughly, it should not find this step difficult. Even people who are not accustomed to prayer should not feel too uncomfortable praying one sentence in this context.

Q7. See especially the details of verses 1–4. Then add any pertinent ideas from verses 5–9.

Q10. A partial answer to this question appears in nearly every verse. Linger on the question long enough for the group to find them all.

Q11. Involve as many group members as possible. (Be sure that they refer to their local congregation of people—not the church building.)

4 / WHAT IS A GOOD FATHER?

1 Corinthians 4

Q1. Discuss this question with your group *before* you read the passage. Encourage more than one response.

Q2. There are several answers in these verses. First, it is God's servant and God's message, therefore it is inappropriate for another to decide whether the job has been done well or not. Second, it was entrusted by God, and an accounting is owed only to God and to no other. Third, the reward will come from God, so an evaluation by others is pointless. Fourth, there is a set and appropriate time for judgment; any other time is jumping the gun. Finally, no one has anything to claim as his or her own, so no one can take credit. Human judgment, even by one's own conscience, is inappropriate.

Q3. There are several answers to this question. Give your group time to find them and encourage their reactions to what they find. Answers should include what it is that will be judged, the timing, and the emphasis on praise.

Q5. Help the group see both sides of the issue: though all that we have that is good comes from God and no person should be excessively lifted up, yet the gift of a leader is from God Himself, given to serve us, and we should appreciate and care for what God gives us in these people.

Q7. b) Have your group review quickly the previous chapters. These give an idea of the Corinthians' values. Remember that they were having a big argument over which teacher was really the best and most prestigious (1:12).

Q8. An honest answer from you as the leader may help group members be more realistic and insightful about their own preferences if they seem to have trouble with this. We each tend to evaluate leaders on superficial merit at times.

Q9. There are a number of characteristics implied. Here are some your group may mention: Paul provides a model for his children to imitate. He warns them of danger. He sends them a helper whom he loves and respects. He longs for them to do well. He gives them time to get things in order before he comes to inspect them, so that he may praise them instead of discipline them.

Q10. These are examples of principles that your group may mention:

verses 1−7: One who is humble and faithful to Scripture.

8−13: He should work hard and be persistent in his trust.

14−21: He should be tender, firm, a good model.

Q11. Bring pencils with you to the discussion, so everyone can take part in this exercise. Share your suggestions about 11c.

5 / WHO CLEANS HOUSE IN GOD'S CHURCH?

1 Corinthians 5

Q1. Group members should note the two reasons suggested in verses 1 and 2 (incest by one man as well as pride about it among the people of the congregation). The group might also use its imagination to infer other reasons for grief based on the succeeding verses.

Q2. Each of these actions and attitudes reveals a more basic misperception of sin. a) "Your boasting" (v. 6). They planned to keep the Festival as though nothing were wrong (v. 8). "And you are proud" (v. 2).

b) See Leviticus 20:11 for Old Testament law regarding incest. See 1 Corinthians 5:1 in reference to Corinthian community standards.

Q3. Examine carefully verses 3−5. Note that Paul claims that even though he is not physically present in such an assembly, he is there in spirit. He says that the power of our Lord Jesus is also present. The outcome of this assembly (v. 5) adds to its solemnity.

Q4. Linger a bit on this question. The danger is more than just that the church will copy this man. Your group should also begin to look at the Corinthian attitude toward sin as shown in verses 6−8.

Be sure to answer both sections of question 4. Notice that the purpose of excommunication is remedial, not punitive. (See the "so that" of verse 5.)

What does Paul mean in verse 5 by "so that the sinful nature may be destroyed" (NIV) or "for the destruction of the flesh" (RSV)? Your group may discuss this at length in answer to the second part of question 4. If they are unable to reach reasonable conclusions after some time, cite Leon Morris:

Two solutions have won support. The one sees in *the flesh* the lower part of man's nature, and takes the passage to mean the destruction of sinful lusts. . . . The other view is that *the flesh* is to be understood as physical, the reference being to sickness and even death. . . .

Though *the flesh* be destroyed it is in order that *the spirit may be saved.* That he means saved in the fullest sense is made clear by the addition *in the day of the Lord.* At the final day of judgment he expects to see the disciplined offender among the Lord's people (Morris, *Tyndale New Testament Commentaries,* pp. 88–89).

Q5. This chapter deals with the painful process of excommunication. To prevent the need for these steps, look at the process by which people are received into your local churches. Should you recommend changes?

Q6. Be sure that your group examines both sides of this contrast, then puts the two together. If they are unable to handle this in a single question, break it into subquestions: What was the Corinthian church's attitude toward sin? (They tolerated, even boasted, about sin.) What was God's attitude about sin? (He says it is like yeast and spreads to the whole batch of dough (v. 6). He sent Christ to die for that sin (v. 7).

Q7. Help your group examine the passage for answers first. They should notice that we are to:

— purify our lives (v. 7).
— grieve over sin (v. 2).
— live up to who we really are (v. 7).
— live in truth and sincerity (v. 9).

After they have done this, guide a discussion on how we might live up to these principles.

Q8. "With such a man do not even eat" (v. 11) probably refers to social eating as well as communion. Leon Morris adds,

When we reflect that our Lord ate with publicans and sinners, and that Paul regards it as permissible to accept invitations to heathen homes (1 Corinthians 10:27), the detailed application of this injunction is not easy. But the principle is plain. There is to be no close fellowship with anyone who claims to be a Christian, but whose life belies his profession (Morris, p. 92).

Q10. Help your group find several responsibilities.

Q12. Getting started on this question may be difficult since it requires us to admit that we have been wrong. You can defuse the tension by mentioning a couple of not-too-embarrassing situations yourself. Family life is full of these. Perhaps someone will then feel free to recall an event of spiritual significance.

6 / TEMPLE ETHICS

1 Corinthians 6

Q1. Use all of the section from 5:12−6:8 for your answers.

Q2. Among other things, he says it is our job to judge those who belong to the church. Since we will one day be called on to judge the world and angels, we should be handling our own disputes now. It is not only inappropriate for Christians to wrangle in front of unbelievers, but Christians should have such care for one another that it rules out this kind of strife. The Corinthians were sinning against ethical standards and against brotherly love.

Q3. Your group should read and comment on each verse individually in answer to this question. Paul has used the situation in the Corinthian church to apply the theology he has been teaching them in previous chapters. He says if these teachings are true, they make a difference in the way the people look at and handle their current problems.

Q4. As you discuss this question, consider obedience to Christian principles, the actions that would lead to a law suit among Christians, the witness to the community, and the special obligations of "brothers" to one another.

Q7. The emphasis in these verses is on a changed relationship with God. In the past they were not sons (inheritors) of God, but among those outside His kingdom. Being outsiders, they behaved like outsiders. Now they have been made fit by God's actions to belong to the kingdom. Paul urges them to live up to their new family name.

Q8. In order to best feel the impact of Paul's comments about our bodies, go straight through these verses mentioning each instance as it occurs.

Q9. Your group needs to see that apparently the Corinthians implied that one bodily function is much like another. Eating is natural and so is fornication. Paul decisively rejects this idea. The belly and food are short-lived; God will do away with both. But the body is destined to be with the Lord for whom it was made; it will be transformed and glorified (Philippians 3:21). There is not a connection between the body and lust as there is between the belly and food. Since God designed the body for Himself, the logical equation is that the body is for *God* in the same way that the belly is for *food*. The belly and the body are for different purposes. Paul uses the word "body" to stand for the whole personality. He views sex as more than the satisfaction of a fleshly need, but as the interaction of whole personalities. Just as food is necessary if the belly is to function and maintain existence, so the Lord is necessary if the body is to function and maintain life. Only God can enable us to live the kind of life for which we were meant (Morris, pp. 99–100). Members of the group needs to work to discover these points for themselves. This note may help you, as leader, clearly see the distinctions, but it is in the text. The individuals in the group will understand and remember it better if they thresh it out fully during the study.

Q10. Mention some contemporary sexual ideas of which your group is aware. These need not be extravagant to be at variance with Paul's teaching—even some of our own views may need reexamining in the light of Paul's premises.

Q11. Having been cleansed, set apart for Christ (sanctified), and made right with God, it seems incongruous to live now as though this had never happened. There is a new understanding of the way my life belongs to and springs from Jesus Christ. Though everything is permissible for me, in that God doesn't count it against me and it will not change my relationship to Him, everything is not helpful to me or to my fellowship with God. It would be foolish to choose a second-rate life.

Q12. Look through all of today's chapter to find the illustrations that answer this question.

7 / SHOULD I STAY SINGLE? GET MARRIED? STAY MARRIED?

1 Corinthians 7

Q1. Read this question before you have the chapter read aloud. After the reading, ask each person present to offer at least one answer.

Q2. Possible answers include:

— Paul says marriage first, sex later; Today says, "You don't need marriage; don't get tied down."

— Paul says our body belongs also to our spouse (vv. 3–4); Today says, "Consider your body your own."

— Paul thinks more of duty than rights. (Sex is my duty to my spouse, rather than my right to demand my own privacy or my own satisfaction); Today says, "My rights come first."

— Paul implies that sex is more than physical (vv. 3–4). This grows out of his "one body" idea of chapter 6; Today says the one-night stand is simply physical recreation.

— Paul says chastity is a gift (v. 7); Today says chastity is weird.

— Paul says to marry if you *don't* have self-control over sexual urges; Today says marry only if you have enough self-control to stay with one person.

— Paul says we should protect ourselves from immorality by getting married; Today says sex outside of marriage is not immoral.

— Paul says a married couple may agree to forgo sex for a brief period in order to spend time in prayer (v. 5); Today finds that unimaginable.

Q3. Mention several effects both positive and negative.

Q6. Of verse 14, *The New Bible Commentary* says,

> *The unbelieving husband is consecrated,* i.e. not 'made personally holy' (cf. 6:11), for he is still unsaved (v. 16), but treated as in a special relationship with God solely for the purpose of the marriage. Children of such a union are similarly covered, presumably until of responsible age. Scripture teaches that divine blessings extend to individuals' children and to their sphere of life (Genesis 17:7; 39:5) .... Paul's aim is doubtless to reassure Christians that there is for them nothing in a mixed marriage contrary to Christian holiness. (Hillyer 1970, p. 1060.)

Q7. As your group works through these uses of the word "called" be sure it notices two general categories: 1) God has *called* us to a station in life; 2) God has *called* us to Himself.

Q8. See verse 19.

Q9. Spend several minutes on this question. Plan for each person present to respond in some way.

Note on verses 36–38 (see question 10 page 50):

Bible translations differ markedly in the wording of these verses. They describe three different relationships. *New International Version* says, "If anyone thinks he is acting improperly toward the virgin he is engaged to . . ." *The Jerusalem Bible* translates these verses, "Still, if there is anyone who feels that it would not be fair to his daughter to let her grow too old for marriage . . ." And the *New English Bible* says, "But if a man has a partner in celibacy and feels that he is not behaving properly towards . . ."

Since Bible translators render this text so many different ways, it is not probable that the group will come to firm conclusions about it. We recommend that your group pass over these three verses.

Q11. See especially verses 26, 29, 31.

Q12. Sample questions appear below, but don't read these to your group. Let them formulate their own as they review the chapter. Then add any ideas they miss from the list below.

— Am I having trouble keeping celibate (vv. 1–9)?

— Could I live with this person until I die (vv. 10–16)?

— Has God called me to marriage (vv. 17–24)?

— Would this person help me keep God's commands (v. 19)?

— Is there a current crisis that ought to influence my decision (vv. 25–31)?

— Could I serve God better as a single person (vv. 32–35)?

— Is my intended partner a Christian (v. 39)?

Q13. Save enough time so that each person who wants to can respond thoughtfully.

8 / HOW CAN I DEVELOP A HEALTHY CONSCIENCE?

1 Corinthians 8

Q1. Name the two sides of this controversy and then find as many descriptive terms for each as you can.

Q2. Pride often accompanies knowledge, but it is often a pride that is the opposite of the genuine Christian spirit. A Christian structure is built up of love. Second, any knowledge we can have here on earth is incomplete, so there is little point in taking pride in, what is at best, partial. Third, love has permanent effects. And fourth, as Leon Morris says, "The really important thing is not that we know God, but that He knows us." Love, not knowledge, should be the determining factor in a Christian's decisions.

Q4, Q5. These questions border on personal application. Question 4 is designed to allow each person in the group to reflect on the attractiveness of God and gain a greater awareness of Him. Question 5, on the other hand, instead of centering on the feelings that move us toward God, looks at more selfish feelings that could distance us from God and from others.

Q6. This question is built on the information in the text, but calls on the imagination of the group member in answering it. What would it be like to be a young, uncertain

Christian, eager to do what is right, but still close to non-Christian values and practices?

Q7. We usually think of our conscience as a rather uncomfortable appendage that keeps us from having a good time. However, a person without a conscience has little stability. Decisions have to be made on a whim-to-whim basis and change according to prevailing emotion. Our consciences keep us on course by helping us know what is good and what is dangerous. Members of your group have undoubtedly experienced personally and observed in others what happens if we persistently act in defiance of our consciences. Since we cannot live in this sort of dissonance, we become confused, irritable, anxious, and we eventually tune out the voice of conscience in order to gain unity and peace.

Q8. Paul lets us know that what is at jeopardy in this issue is nothing less than our fellowship with Christ. The weak person is not just anyone, but our brother or sister, cared for by no less a person than Christ Himself; His caring took the form of action, one as costly as His death. No one is unimportant enough to be scorned. And our decision at another's expense is of great consequence even though it may be one of little importance to us; it could mean that person's destruction.

Q9. Consider these questions in order to describe the two kinds of Christians: 1) How are they different? 2) How are they alike? 3) Which has the greater responsibility? Why?

Q11. Paul is not disparaging knowledge, but is giving it a fuller meaning.

Q12. Use the principles in this passage as guidelines to concrete suggestions. Some answers might include: to study Scripture, have good teachers, and enter into group study and discussion.

9 / RIGHTS AND DISCIPLINE

1 Corinthians 9

Q1. See primarily verses 1 and 2.

Q2. See verses 3–6, 12, and 14.

Q5. If people are present who can't remember the main thrust of chapter 8, summarize it briefly outlining the principle reasons given there for limiting personal freedom.

Q6. Notice the contrast between Paul's words, "Am I not free?" in verse 1 and the limitations he has placed on himself in verses 15–19.

In discussing question 6, your group might benefit from looking at the relationship between the way Paul uses the words "rights," "voluntary," "free," and "compelled."

Q7. Linger long enough on this question for several to explore it in a meaningful way.

Q11. You can put this question in broader perspective by reviewing 1 Corinthians 8:9 and the answers to today's question 5.

Q12. Wait for at least a couple of people to speak honestly in answer to this question. Be ready to talk about at least one area of needed discipline in your own life.

10 / DO *ALL* TO THE GLORY OF GOD?

1 Corinthians 10

Q1. Find out what happened to "all," to "most," and to only "some" of the people.

Q2. The flow of thought throughout the passage helps answer this question, but verses 1, 5, and 6 are most explicit.

Q3. These first ten verses are full of references to the history of the people of Israel. You will not have time to read these passages in the study, but should be prepared to summarize them for the group. The first five verses refer to incidents recounted in Exodus 13:21; 14:21, 22, 29; 16:4, 35;17:6. There are four Old Testament references that show examples of the actions referred to in 1 Corinthians 10:6–10. They are Exodus 32:4–6 (idolatry); Numbers 25:1–9 (immorality); Numbers 21:4–9 (testing); and Numbers 16:41–49 (grumbling). These last four references are the most important in answering this question.

Q4. a) Look back at the first five verses. b) Keep an eye on the clock as you develop this question. Most of your study yet remains.

Q8. This act looks both toward union with Christ and union with other Christians.

Q9. *The New Bible Commentary* published by InterVarsity Press has this to say about verses 19–22:

> Paul is not implying by the illustration that idol's food is anything other than food, or that a stone or wooden idol has any reality (cf. 8:4f.). But communion can be only with the living. Thus what pagans sacrifice, whether they realize it or not, they offer to demons (cf. Deuteronomy 32:17), who take advantage of men's leaning towards idolatry. Paul would save the Corinthians from being unwitting partners with demons. On such an issue there can be no compromise. Fellowship with the Lord and fellowship with demons are utterly incompatible. Consequently to join in heathen festivities is inevitably to provoke the Lord to jealousy (cf. Deuteronomy 32:21), for devotion to Him must be exclusive (Hillyer 1970, p. 1064).

Q13. Make the lists before looking ahead to the rest of the question. When considering changes ask if some jobs should be eliminated or others added.

11 / PRIVATE BATTLES WITH PUBLIC WORSHIP

1 Corinthians 11

Q1. Verses 4 and 5 assume, without criticism, that both men and women pray and prophesy in public.

Note: The word "prophesy" of verse 3 does not necessarily mean foretelling the future. "It is used with the primary meaning of telling forth the Divine counsel." (W. E. Vine, *An Expository Dictionary of New Testament Words,* Old Tappan, New Jersey: Fleming H. Revell Co., 1940. p. 222.)

This would come close to our practice of teaching God's word through Scripture and exhorting people to obey it.

Q3. Paul refers to at least four areas of authority: social custom (vv. 4–5), biblical and theological reasons (v. 7–10), natural order (v. 14), and church practice (v. 16). Encourage people to sort these out for themselves, but if they do not discover all four within a reasonable period, point them out. They will need them as a basis for the next three questions.

Q4. Don't expect members to find total agreement as they interpret these verses, but do try to keep them rooted in the passage as they struggle with modern–day differences.

Q7. See verses 17–22.

Q8. Your group should speak of the Corinthians' attitude toward each other, toward Christ, and toward the sacrament.

Q9. Notice particularly the following phrases: "which is for you" (v. 24), "new covenant" (v. 25), "proclaim the Lord's death" (v. 26), "until he comes" (v. 26). Even "on the night he was betrayed" (v. 23) implies that Jesus set up this ceremony with full knowledge that He was about to die, but that His death, though voluntary, was with great purpose.

Q10. Encourage personal responses. This is an opportunity for the person who is coming close to accepting Christ's death for his personal redemption to say so. It is also an opportunity for the person who has already taken that step to share its meaning with the group.

Q11. Refer to verses 27–34 first, then draw in information from the entire section. Answers should include:

— appropriate worship setting.

— awareness of and consideration for other participants.

— recognition of the price Christ paid.

— acknowledgment that it was "for me," that this establishes a new relationship with God.

— corporate witness to each other and to the outside community.

— reminder that this ceremony is temporary, that Christ is coming again.

— self-examination: how should I live in view of this new covenant?

— awe of the judgment of the Lord.

— a review of my life that takes in my sicknesses and hardships. Ask, "Is this the Lord's discipline? Do I need to reorganize my life to make it more in tune with God?

Q12. See verses 30–33.

Q13. Allow enough time for your group to thoughtfully consider and discuss these questions.

12 / BODY LANGUAGE

1 Corinthians 12

Q1. Some of the most important things your group should discover in the passage are: the Spirit emphasizes Jesus as the Lord; He gives a variety of gifts and leaves no one out; He is the One who determines who gets what gifts; He intends these gifts to be used for the good of all believers.

Q2. Use all eleven verses, being sure to notice the answers in verse 11. You should be able to find four or five, including the fact that all Christians call Jesus, Lord (Master), worship the same God, and have at least one spiritual gift.

Q3. Discuss several ways that Christians are different from one another. Several are mentioned in the passage: we have different kinds of gifts, different ways of using our gifts, and different services that we perform. Group members can probably think of ways to say these in their own words and give examples.

Q6. Use concepts from all of this section (v. 1–11).

Q7. There are some important ways in which the human body and the church are alike. Paul emphasizes that though it is made of many parts, it is still a single unit; the parts cannot function separately. There is a single organizing "head" and one animating spirit. Unity and diversity are essential characteristics of both the human body and the body of Christ.

Q8. The group should mention the two attitudes that characterize the problems: "I don't belong" and "I don't need you." But this question asks for more than labeling; have the group go on to describe each situation in somewhat more detail.

Q10. If you have trouble getting answers to this question or have time to explore it further, you might choose to use this question: What are some of the gifts you consider less important?

Q11. It is important for the group to see that this passage stands against the spirit of individualism so dear to us. The basic teaching is that we Christians are one body and stand or fall together. Evidently God intended us to learn to depend on each other and cherish one another. The basic unity of the body of Christ, despite its great diversity, is the repeated emphasis throughout this chapter—verses 7, 12–14, 20, and

24–25. We are strong on individuality and freedom and on a personal relationship with God; so we often fail to see that we are one in many essential ways.

Q12. Knowing that Jesus is Lord helps me put gifts into perspective. It is hard to be puffed up about my own gift, if it is no more necessary than each other gift and if it cannot operate effectively alone. It is more difficult to be jealous if God has given all gifts for my good. It is harder for me to sit on the sidelines or be preoccupied with my own concerns if I am responsible to Jesus the Lord for what I do with the gift He has given. With all the diversity of gifts given the church, it could be confusing to get them working together effectively if we didn't have a Head to help us put it all together.

13 / IS MY LOVE GOD'S LOVE?

1 Corinthians 13

Q3. A thorough discussion of this question could fill up the remainder of your study time if you dig deeply back into chapter 12. Allow a reasonable time for discussion, then proceed to the next question.

Q6. Be sure answers to the third question refer to both patience and kindness. Some situations call for patience and others call for kindness. Your group should distinguish between these two demonstrations of love.

Q8. Verse 7 must be tempered by verse 6. There is a truth; there is also evil. The "endurance" of verse 7 assumes a judgment between these two extremes, with love taking the side of and rejoicing in truth.

Q9. Allow several minutes for silent prayer. (Give enough time to permit real communication with God.) Just tell the members of your group that they need not feel uncomfortable with these silent minutes. They should use the time to search their hearts and pray. Close this silent time with a simple, "In Jesus' name, Amen."

Q10. Explore the many details in these verses.

Q12. Expect several people to participate in this application question.

14 / AM I GOD'S GIFT TO MY CHURCH?

1 Corinthians 14

Q1. As you start your own study of this chapter, it may be of some help to have an overview of this section of Paul's letter in mind starting with chapter 12. Reread this, noticing that in chapter 12, Paul showed that though there were a variety of gifts given to the church, the essential unity of the members possessing these gifts undergirded all. He went on in chapter 13 to show that love is preeminent above all else. Now he is in a position to deal specifically with the question of tongues. He is careful to be clear that the gift is legitimate and desirable, but restrains the exaggerated importance the Corinthians had placed on it.

Note that the principle underlying Paul's instruction is still that the growth and unity of the church is of first importance in the exercise of the gifts of the Holy Spirit.

Though both tongues and prophecy are mentioned in these first five verses, the emphasis is on prophecy. Encourage the members of your group to follow the flow of the passage (and the flow of the questions) to help them understand Paul's emphasis here.

Q2. After finding the illustrations (there are three), have your group members state as precisely as possible, in their own words, the differing point of each illustration.

Q3. Use the whole passage, verses 1–12.

Q5. As group members label or describe Paul's attitude toward the gift of tongues, have them indicate what parts of this passage lead them to use their particular description.

Q10. As you read, imagine you are present. Make yourself alert to the sights and sounds. Mention as many as possible.

Note on verses 34–36: The meaning of these instructions by Paul on the role of the Corinthian women in worship is still disputed by Bible scholars. Paul has previously in this letter assumed that women would prophesy in church, and he did not criticize them for it (1 Corinthians 11:5). Also, at Pentecost, as recorded in Acts 2:17–18, both men and women received the gift of prophecy in fulfillment of the prophecy of Joel 2:28–29. Many believe Paul gave these commands for cultural reasons. They say the command to silence meant only that women were not to engage in idle chatter or disruptive questions but should be aware of the need for emancipated Christian women to avoid unnecessary criticism by flouting social convention. Other commentators take the instructions at face value: Women are not to speak in a worship service either then or now.

In view of the long history of disagreement by notable scholars over the interpretation of these verses, we recommend that you not spend undue time on them. A definitive answer during your hour together seems unlikely.

15 / HOW WILL IT END?

1 Corinthians 15

Q1. Your group should point out the following words: Christ, died, sins, Scriptures, buried, raised, third day, appeared.

A short reason for the importance of each word is sufficient here. Several will be treated later in the study. Someone should point out that the words "buried" and "third day" speak strongly that Jesus was really dead, not just unconscious.

Q2. Verses 5–8 provide a selective list of six individuals or groups who saw and recognized Jesus after the Resurrection. Two of these, James and Paul, were not even believers during Christ's ministry. In addition, Paul points out in verses 9–11, that he and all the other apostles had always preached the Resurrection as part of the Christian faith—and the Corinthians had believed it.

Q3. Group members should point out the following:

— Christ was not raised (vv. 13, 16, 17).
— Preaching is useless (v. 14).
— Your faith is useless (v. 14).
— We are false witnesses about God (v. 15).
— God didn't raise Christ (v. 17).
— Your faith is futile (v. 17).
— You are still in your sins (v. 17).
— Those believers who have already died are lost (v. 18).
— We ought to be pitied more than all men (v. 19).

Q5. See verse 20.

Q6. See verses 20–28.

Q8. Note the facts of verses 29–34. Then from these details, discuss the freedom of thought and action that stems from belief in life after death. Someone should also mention the restrictions that grow out of the certainty of judgment to come. On the side of unbelief, your group should comment on at least the transitory pleasure of "Eat and drink for tomorrow we die."

Q12. Verses 50–57. "Sleep" (v. 51) means "die." In other words, those who are alive at the time of Christ's return will not be left out of the transformation of resurrection. For further information about that event, see 1 Thessalonians 4:13–18.

Q14, Q15. Leave adequate time for most of your group members to enter a thoughtful discussion of these application questions.

16 / UNTIL I COME . . .

1 Corinthians 16

Q1. Use your maps as you notice the people and places mentioned in the passage. Be sure to include verses 10–11 as you discuss 1b.

Q2. Use all twelve verses. a) Even Paul's instructions about the collection of a gift for another church show real concern for his Corinthian friends. b) Be sure your group answers this portion thoughtfully since the next question is one that applies the principles you discover as you answer this question. As part of your discussion, consider when, how much, and for what purpose.

Q5. This question is a review question of 1 Corinthians. Give each person in your group one or two chapters to scan before attempting to answer it.

Q6. Find at least seven or eight commands. In the second part of this question, find at least one situation that might have been helped by obeying Paul's instruction here. (This question will be easier to handle if you have scanned the book of 1 Corinthians in the manner suggested for the previous question.)

Q7. Some answers to this question include the greeting to Priscilla and Aquila, the encouragement to greet each other with a holy kiss, to be united, to submit to those who labor for the church, to love the Lord.

8. You may need to point the group back into the passage. Paul mentions some expression of love in nearly every verse. Help the group use the examples in the passage and personalize them with concrete, specific suggestions.

BIBLIOGRAPHY

Hillyer, Norman. "1 Corinthians." *New Bible Commentary,* edited by D. Guthrie, J. A. Motyer, A. M. Stibbs, D. J. Wiseman. Downers Grove: InterVarsity Press, 1970.

Morris, Leon. *The First Epistle of Paul to the Corinthians.* Tyndale New Testament Commentaries, edited by R.V.G. Tasker. Grand Rapids: Wm. B. Eerdmans Publishing Co., 1958.

Vine, W. E. *An Expository Dictionary of New Testament Words.* Old Tappan, N. J.: Fleming H. Revell Co., 1940.